THE STORY OF MY CHILDHOOD

BY

CLARA BARTON

NEW YORK
THE BAKER & TAYLOR CO.
1907

Copyright, 1907, by
THE JOURNAL PUBLISHING CO.,
Meriden, Conn.

THE JOURNAL PRESS.

Clara Barton

PRESIDENT OF THE NATIONAL ASSOCIATION OF THE FIRST AID OF AMERICA.

Photograph taken on the occasion of the First Annual Meeting of the above
Association, held in Boston, June 7, 1906.

THE STORY OF MY CHILDHOOD.

PREFACE

Dear Miss Clara Barton:

Our classes in The History of the United States are studying about you, and we want to know more.

Our teacher says she has seen you. That you live in, or near Washington, District of Columbia, and that, although very busy, she thought you might be willing to receive a short letter from us, and I write to ask you to be so kind as to tell us what you did when you were a little girl like us. All of us want to know. I am almost thirteen.

If you could send us a few words, we should all be very happy. I write for all.

Your little girl friend,

MARY ST. CLARE,
* * * New York.

October third, nineteen hundred, six.

Miss Clara Barton:

I am studying about you in my History, and what you did in the war, and I thought I would write and ask you what you did afore you did that.

Yours truly,

JAMES C. HAMLIN.

* * * Center, Iowa,
May 24th, 1906.

Dear Children of the Schools:

Your oft-repeated appeals have reached
me. They are too many and too earnest
to be disregarded; and because of them,
and because of my love for you, I have
dedicated this little book to you. I have
made it small, that you may the more easily
read it. I have done it in the hope that
it may give you pleasure, and in the wish
that, when you shall be women and men,
you may each remember, as I do, that you
were once a child, full of childish thoughts
and action, but of whom it was said, "Suffer them to come unto Me, and forbid
them not, for of such is the Kingdom of
Heaven."

Faithfully your friend,

CLARA BARTON.

Glen Echo, Maryland,
May twenty-ninth, 1907.

THE STORY OF MY CHILDHOOD.

I T was May—the cherry trees were in
bloom. For the first time in three
years I had been able to sit for an
evening among a company of persons (invalids like myself seeking
strength), trying to entertain them
with some remembrances of bygone
days. I see it still, the broad parlor of
that grand old "Hillside Home," the
mother and inspiration of all the hun-
dreds of sanitariums and health re-
storing institutions of the country to-
day. I had made my home near it, at
the foot of the blossoming orchard.

Down among the trees and twitter-
ing robins next morning came one of
my listeners; a broad-shouldered,
manly looking man, the face so full of
benign intelligence that once seen was
never to be forgotten. He came in at
the open door, merrily shaking off the
cherry blossoms like large flakes of
early snow, an entire stranger to me
until the previous evening. He seated
himself and entered into conversation
with a familiar ease that bespoke the
cultured gentleman. After a few
minutes he turned earnestly to me
with: "Miss Barton, I have an errand
in coming to you. I have a request
to make."

I said I hoped I should be able to
comply. He hesitated, as if thinking
how to commence, but at length said:
"I want you to recall and write the

first thing you remember—the first event that made sufficient impression upon you to be remembered."

I waited in silence and he went on:

"And then I want you to write the next, and then the next, and so on, until you have written all—everything connected with yourself and your life that you can recall. I want it; we want it; the world wants it, and again I ask you to do it. Can you promise me?"

His earnest manner demanded an earnest reply. I could not promise to do it, but would promise to consider it.

This was in the spring of 1876. I have never forgotten the request through all these thirty-one busy years, and have carefully kept the promise to consider it; and to-night take my

pencil to describe the first moment of
my life that I remember.

By the dates I must have been
nearly two and a half years old, for
I was born on Christmas day, and
now the lilacs were in bloom. It was
a rather newly built country house
where I had commenced my earthly
pilgrimage, and being the youngest by
a dozen or so years, of a family of two
brothers and two sisters, I naturally
lacked child playmates and was left
much to my own entertainment.

On this occasion I must have been
enjoying a ramble by myself in the
grass-green dooryard, with the broad
hand-hewn doorstep and the traditional lilacs on either side. Suddenly
my resounding cries brought the
whole family to the door in alarm.
My wailing took the form of a com-

MY BIRTHPLACE.

plaint expressed with my best lin-
guistic ability:

"Baby los' 'im—pitty bird—baby
los' 'im—baby mos' caught him—pitty
bird—baby mos' caught 'im."

At length they succeeded in induc-
ing me to listen to a question, "But
where did it go, Baby?"

Among my heart-breaking sobs I
pointed to a small round hole under
the doorstep.   The terrified scream of
my mother remained in my memory
forever more.   Her baby had "mos'
caught" a snake.

I recall nothing more for nearly
a year and a half, when my terrors
again took possession.   An esteemed
and greatly beloved relative of the
family had died.   The funeral ser-
vices were to be held four miles away.
All the household would attend ex-

cepting myself and the younger of my
two brothers, David, some sixteen
years old, who was deputed to act as
body guard, doubtless under strict
orders.

I can picture the large family sitting room with its four open windows,
which room I was not to leave, and
my guardian was to remain near me.
Some outside duty called him from
the house and I was left to my own
observations. A sudden thunder
shower came up; massive rifts of
clouds rolled up in the east, and the
lightning darted among them like
blazing fires. The thunder gave them
language and my terrified imagination
endowed them with life.

Among the animals of the farm was
a huge old ram, that doubtless upon
some occasion had taught me to re-

spect him, and of which I had a mortal fear.   My terrors transformed those rising, rolling clouds into a whole heaven full of angry rams, marching down upon me. Again my screams alarmed, and the poor brother, conscience stricken that he had left his charge, rushed breathless in, to find me on the floor in hysterics, a condition of things he had never seen; and neither memory nor history relate how either of us got out of it.

In these later years I have observed that writers of sketches, in a friendly desire to compliment me, have been wont to dwell upon my courage, representing me as personally devoid of fear, not even knowing the feeling. However correct that may have become, it is evident I was not constructed that way, as in the earlier

years of my life I remember nothing
but fear.

There can be no doubt that my advent into the family was at least a
novelty, as the last before me was a
beautiful blue-eyed, curly-haired little
girl of a dozen summers. That the
event was probably looked for with
interest is shadowed in the fact of
preparations made for it. The still
existing few pieces in my possession
testify to the purchase of a full, com-
plete and withal rather aristocratic
dinner set of "Old Willow," which
did faithful service many years; and
the remaining bits of dainty pink and
white, tell of the tea set to match,
in the cups of which were told the future of many a merry party that
learned their reality through still later
years, not all pink and white.

I became the seventh member of a household consisting of the father and mother, two sisters and two brothers, each of whom for his and her intrinsic merits and special characteristics deserves an individual history, which it shall be my conscientious duty to portray as far as possible as these pages progress. For the present it is enough to say that each one manifested an increasing personal interest in the newcomer, and as soon as developments permitted, set about instructing her in the various directions most in accord with the tastes and pursuits of each.

Of the two sisters, the elder was already a teacher. The younger followed soon, and naturally my book education became their first care, and under these conditions it is little to say, that I have no knowledge of ever learning to read, or of a time that I did not do my own story reading. The other studies followed very early.

My elder brother, Stephen, was a noted mathematician. He inducted me into the mystery of figures. Multiplication, division, subtraction, halves, quarters and wholes, soon ceased to be a mystery, and no toy equalled my little slate. But the younger brother (he of the thunder storm and hysterics) had entirely other tastes, and would have none of these things. My father was a lover of horses, and one of the first in the vicinity to introduce blooded stock. He had large lands, for New England. He raised his own colts; and Highlanders, Virginians and Morgans pranced the fields in idle contempt of the solid old farm horses.

Of my brother, David, to say that
he was fond of horses describes nothing; one could almost add that he was
fond of nothing else.   He was the
Buffalo Bill of the surrounding country, and here commences his part of
my education.   It was his delight to
take me, a little girl five years old, to
the field, seize a couple of those beautiful young creatures, broken only to
the halter and bit, and gathering the
reins of both bridles firmly in hand,
throw me upon the back of one colt,
spring upon the other himself, and
catching me by one foot, and bidding
me "cling fast to the mane," gallop
away over field and fen, in and out
among the other colts in wild glee like
ourselves.   They were merry rides we
took.   This was my riding school.   I
never had any other, but it served me

well. To this day my seat on a saddle or on the back of a horse is as se-
cure and tireless as in a rocking chair,
and far more pleasurable.   Sometimes, in later years, when I found
myself suddenly on a strange horse
in a trooper's saddle, flying for life or
liberty in front of pursuit, I blessed
the baby lessons of the wild gallops
among the beautiful colts.

Various as were the topics of instruction pursued by my youthful
teachers, my father had still others.
He was "Captain" Stephen Barton,
had served as a non-commissioned officer, under General Wayne (Mad An-
thony) in the French and Indian Wars
on the then Western frontiers.   His
soldier habits and tastes never left
him.   Those were also strong politi-

cal days—Andrew Jackson days—and
very naturally my father became my
instructor in military and political lore.
I listened breathlessly to his war
stories. Illustrations were called for,
and we made battles and fought them.
Every shade of military etiquette was
regarded. Generals, colonels, cap-
tains and sergeants were given their
proper place and rank. So with the
political world; the president, cab-
inet and leading officers of the govern-
ment were learned by heart, and
nothing gratified the keen humor of
my father more than the parrot-like
readiness with which I lisped these
often difficult names, and the accu-
racy with which I repeated them upon
request. My elder sister, with a
teacher's intuition, mistrusting that
my ideas on these points might be

somewhat vague, confidentially drew
from me one day my impressions in
regard to the personages whose names
I handled so glibly, and to the amuse-
ment of the family found that I had
no conception of their being men like
other men, but had invested them
with miraculous size and importance.
I thought the president might be as
large as the meeting house, and the
vice-president perhaps the size of the
school house. And yet I am not going to say that even this instruction
had never any value for me. When
later, I, like all the rest of our country people, was suddenly thrust into
the mysteries of war, and had to find
and take my place and part in it, I
found myself far less a stranger to
the conditions than most women, or
even ordinary men for that matter;

I never addressed a colonel as captain, got my cavalry on foot, or mounted my infantry.

My mother, like the sensible woman that she was, seeming to conclude that there were plenty of instructors without her, attempted very little, but rather regarded the whole thing as a sort of mental conglomeration, and looked on with a kind of amused curiosity to see what they would make of it. Indeed, I heard her remark many years after, that I came out with a more level head than she would have thought possible.

My first individual ownership was "Button." In personality (if the term be admissible), Button represented a sprightly, medium-sized, very white dog, with silky ears, sparkling black eyes and a very short tail. His bark spoke for itself. Button belonged to me. No other claim was instituted, or ever had been. It was said that on my entrance into the family, Button constituted himself my guardian. He watched my first steps and tried to pick me up when I fell down. One was never seen without the other. He proved an apt and obedient pupil, obeying me precept upon precept, if not line upon line. He stood on two feet to ask for his food, and made a bow on receiving it, walked on three legs when very lame, and so on, after the manner of his crude instruction; went everywhere with me through the day, waited patiently while I said my prayers and continued his guard on the foot of the bed at night. Button shared my board as well as my bed.

This fact gave opportunity for an amusing bit of sport for the family at my expense, as was their wont.

One would, with considerable ado (to lend importance to the occasion), make me a present of some divisible luxury, as cake or candies. This called, on my part, for positive orders to all to sit down and share my gift with me, as I never partook of it alone. A line or circle was formed, comprising the entire family, Button occupying the last seat. I then proceeded to make a careful hand count of each, including Button; then retired and accurately divided my gift, a piece for each, but not myself, as I was not in the count. I then went and gave a piece to every one. The fun came in watching the silent wonderment and resignation with which I contemplated my own empty hands, a condition of things I could not at all comprehend, but made no complaint. Of course, each in generous sympathy offered to give back to me his or her piece; but here came in my careful mother's protest and command, so seldom heard. "No," I must not be taught to think I could give a thing and still possess it, or its value. A gift must be outright. I must do earnestly all that I did. Each might generously give me back a very small piece, to make in all no more than would have been my share, and I must be made to understand that even this was a favor and not a right. I then went around and received my crumbs. This all went well till I came to Button. When I held out my hand for his little charity, he had nothing for me. I could never understand this discourtesy of Button.

This was one of the many jokes reserved for me as I grew older. But far above and beyond it all, as the years sped on, and the hands were still, shone the gleam of the far-sighted mother's watchfulness that neither toil could obscure, nor mirth relax.

My home instruction was by no means permitted to stand in the way of the "regular school," which consisted of two terms each year, of three months each. The winter term included not only the large boys and girls, but in reality the young men and young women of the neighborhood. An exceptionally fine teacher often drew the daily attendance of advanced scholars for several miles. Our district had this good fortune. I introduce with pleasure and with reverence the name of Richard Stone; a firmly-set, handsome young man of twenty-six or seven, of commanding figure and presence, combining all the elements of a teacher with a discipline never questioned. His glance of disapproval was a reprimand, his frown something he never needed to go beyond. The love and respect of his pupils exceeded even their fear. It was no uncommon thing for summer teachers to come twenty miles to avail themselves of the winter term of "Col." Stone, for he was a high militia officer, and at that young age was a settled man with a family of four little children. He had married at eighteen.

I am thus particular in my description of him, both because of my childish worship of him, and because I shall have occasion to refer to him later. The opening of his first term was a signal for the Barton family, and seated on the strong shoulders of my stalwart brother Stephen, I was taken a mile through the tall drifts to school. I have often questioned if in this movement there might not have been a touch of mischievous curiosity on the part of these not at all dull youngsters, to see what my performance at school might be.

I was, of course, the baby of the school. I recall no introduction to the teacher, but was set down among the many pupils in the by no means spacious room, with my spelling book and the traditional slate, from which nothing could separate me. I was seated on one of the low benches and sat very still. At length the majestic schoolmaster seated himself, and taking a primer, called the class of little ones to him. He pointed the letters to each. I named them all, and was asked to spell some little words, "dog," "cat," etc., whereupon I hesitatingly informed him that I did "not spell there." "Where do you spell?" "I spell in 'Artichoke,'" that being the leading word in the three syllable column in my speller. He good naturedly conformed to my suggestion, and I was put into the "artichoke" class to bear my part for the winter, and read and "spell for the head." When, after a few weeks, my brother Stephen was declared by the committee to be too advanced for a common school, and was placed in charge of an important school himself, my unique transportation devolved upon the other brother, David.

No colts now, but solid wading through the high New England drifts. The Rev. Mr. Menseur of the Episcopal church of Leicester, Mass., if I recollect aright, wisely comprehending the grievous inadaptability of the school books of that time, had compiled a small geography and atlas suited to young children, known as Menseur's Geography. It was a novelty, as well as a beneficence; nothing of its kind having occurred to makers of the school books of that day. They seemed not to have recognized the existence of a state of childhood in the intellectual creation. During the winter I had become the happy possessor of a Menseur's Geography

and Atlas. It is questionable if my
satisfaction was fully shared by others of the household. I required a
great deal of assistance in the study
of my maps, and became so interested
that I could not sleep, and was not
willing that others should, but persisted in waking my poor drowsy sister in the cold winter mornings to sit
up in bed and by the light of a tallow
candle, help me to find mountains, riv-
ers, counties, oceans, lakes, islands,
isthmuses, channels, cities, towns and
capitals.

The next May the summer school
opened, taught by Miss Susan Tor-
rey. Again, I write the name rever-
ently, as gracing one of the most
perfect of personalities. I was not
alone in my childish admiration,
for her memory remained a living

reality in the town long years after
the gentle spirit fled.   My sisters
were both teaching other schools, and
I must make my own way, which I
did, walking a mile with my one pre-
cious little schoolmate, Nancy Fitts.
Nancy Fitts! The playmate of my
childhood; the "chum" of laughing
girlhood; the faithful trusted companion of young womanhood, and the beloved life friend that the relentless
grasp of time has neither changed, nor
taken from me.

On entering the wide open door of
the inviting schoolhouse, armed with
some most unsuitable reader, a
spelling book, geography, atlas and
slate, I was seized with an intense fear
at finding myself with no member of
the family near, and my trepidation
became so visible that the gentle teach-

er, relieving me of my burden of books, took me tenderly on her lap and did her best to reassure and calm me. At length I was given my seat, with a desk in front for my atlas and slate, my toes at least a foot from the floor, and that became my daily, happy home for the next three months.

I partially recall an event which occurred when I was five years old; the incidents which I could not have personally remembered, must have been supplied by later relations. It seems that I was suddenly discovered to be alarmingly ill. In response to the terror of the moment, the saddle was thrown on Black Stallion, the king of the herd, his rough rider mounted and away for the doctor, on "Oxford Plain," five miles away. "Not at

home—out on a professional drive."
Followed to "Sutton Street," six miles
further on. "Gone." Back over "Hog
Hill" and across the town to the west.
At length overtaken and brought back
at a speed little less than that which
had called him, for the doctor was a
fearless driver. The thunder of the
flying hoofs and the speed of the rider as they passed had alarmed the people.   All the town knew the horse
and the rider, and knew as well that
something bad had happened at Captain Barton's.   Men dropped their
work, harnessed their own teams and
drove with all haste to see if, per-
chance, it were anything in which they
could help. When the doctor arrived,
the yard and road were filled with
people, waiting his coming and diag-
nosis.

Shortly the verbal bulletin went out:
"A sudden, unaccountable and probably fatal attack of bloody dysentery
and convulsions." There was no
more for the sympathetic neighbors
to do; they turned sadly away, and
with them went the report that Captain and Mrs. Barton had lost their
little baby girl.

Of all this I have, naturally, no recollection—neither do I know the lapse
of time till memory again got hold;
but her first grasp of the event was
this: I had occupied as a bed a great
cradle which had been made for some
grown invalid, and preserved in the
household. I was bolstered up in
this cradle, with a little low table at
the side on which was my first meal
of solid food. How I had previously
been nourished I do not know, but I

CAPTAIN STEPHEN BARTON,
MY FATHER.

SALLY STONE BARTON,
MY MOTHER.

can see this meal as clearly as if it had been yesterday. A piece of brown bread crust, about two inches square, rye and Indian, baked on the oven bottom; a tiny wine glass, my Christmas gift, full of home-made blackberry cordial, and a wee bit of my mother's well cured old cheese. There was no need to caution me to eat slowly; knowing that I could have no more, and in dread of coming to the last morsel, I nibbled and sipped and swallowed till I mercifully fell asleep from exhaustion.

There are a good many men over the country who would readily believe that sometimes, at the end of a long fast, food might have tasted very good to me, as it did to them; but no food through the longest fast, ever had the relish of that brown bread crust; and no royal table has ever been so kingly as that where I presided alone over my own feast.

Of the succeeding years, six, seven and eight, I recall little of note beyond my studies, excepting a propensity I indulged for writing verses, many of which were preserved to amuse, others to tease me for many years. Colonel Stone had closed his series of common schools, and opened a special institution on "Oxford Plain," known as the "Oxford High School." Its fame had spread for miles around, and it was regarded as the *Ultima Thule* for teachers, and in a manner a stepping stone or opening door to Harvard and Yale.

My brother Stephen had succeeded Col. Stone in the winter terms of the

home school, and my sisters mainly
had charge of them in summer. Thus
six months of each year offered little
change, the others were long vaca-
tions in which the out-of-doors played
by far the most prominent part. There
were garden and flower beds to be
made, choice pet animals to look after, a few needy families with little
children to be thought of, and some
sewing to be attempted. These latter were in accordance with my mother's recommendations.   I recall no
season of dolls, and believe they were
never included in my curriculum.

Meantime, I fell heir to my mother's side saddle, a beautiful piece of
workmanship, and with some difficulty
learned to adjust myself to it, a rather
useless adjustment it seemed to me at
the time, which opinion I still entertain.

These were years of change in the family. My brothers had become of age and were young men of strength, character and enterprise. They had "bought out" as the term went, the two large farms of my father, and commenced business in earnest for themselves. My father had purchased another farm of some three hundred acres, a few miles nearer the center of the town.

This was a place of note, having been one of the points used for security against the Indians by the old Huguenot Settlers of Oxford, and which has made the town historic. Their main defense was on "Fort Hill," several miles to the east. I was naturally greatly interested in the changes, and doubtless gave them all the time I could spare from my increasing studies. I can recollect even now that my life seemed very full for a little girl of eight years.

During the preceding winter I began to hear talk of my going away to school, and it was decided that I be sent to Col. Stone's High school, to board in his family and go home occasionally. This arrangement, I learned in later years, had a double object. I was what is known as a bashful child, timid in the presence of other persons, a condition of things found impossible to correct at home. In the hope of overcoming this undesirable *mauvais honte*, it was decided to throw me among strangers.

How well I remember my advent. My father took me in his carriage with a little dressing case which I dignified with the appellation of "trunk" —something I had never owned. It was April—cold and bare. The house and school rooms adjoined, and seemed enormously large. The household was also large. The long family table with the dignified preceptor, my loved and feared teacher at three years, at its head, seemed to me something formidable. There were probably one hundred and fifty pupils daily in the ample school rooms, of which I was perhaps the youngest, except the colonel's own children.

My studies were chosen with great care. I remember among them, ancient history with charts. The lessons were learned to repeat by rote. I found difficulty both in learning the proper names and in pronouncing them, as I had not quite outgrown my

lisp. One day I had studied very
hard on the Ancient Kings of Egypt,
and thought I had everything perfect,
and when the pupil above me failed
to give the name of a reigning king,
I answered very promptly that it was
"Potlomy." The colonel checked
with a glance the rising laugh of the
older members of the class, and told
me, very gently, that the P was silent
in that word. I had, however, seen
it all, and was so overcome by mortification for my mistake, and grati-
tude for the kindness of my teacher,
that I burst into tears and was permitted to leave the room.

I am not sure that I was really
homesick, but the days seemed very
long, especially Sundays. I was in
constant dread of doing something
wrong, and one Sunday afternoon I

was sure I had found my occasion. It was early spring. The tender leaves had put out and with them the buds and half open blossoms of the little cinnamon roses, an unfailing ornamentation of a well kept New England home of that day. The children of the family had gathered in the front yard, admiring the roses and daring to pick each a little bouquet. As I stood holding mine, the heavy door at my back swung open, and there was the colonel, in his long, light dressing gown and slippers, direct from his study. A kindly spoken "come with me, Clara," nearly took my last breath. I followed his strides through all the house, up the long flights of stairs, through the halls of the school rooms, silently wondering what I had done more than the oth-

COLONEL RICHARD C. STONE,
MY TEACHER AT THREE YEARS OF AGE.

ers. I knew he was by no means
wont to spare his own children. I had
my handful of roses—so had they.
I knew it was very wrong to have
picked them, but why more wrong for
me than for the others? At length,
and it seemed to me an hour, we
reached the colonel's study, and there,
advancing to meet us, was the Rev-
erend Mr. Chandler, the pastor of our
Universalist church, whom I knew
well.   He greeted me very politely
and kindly, and handed the large, open
school reader which he held, to the
colonel, who put it into my hands,
placed me a little in front of them, and
pointing to a column of blank verse,
very gently directed me to read it. It
was   an   extract   from   Campbell's
"Pleasures of Hope," commencing,
"Unfading hope, when life's last em-

bers burn." I read it to the end, a page
or two. When finished, the good pastor came quickly and relieved me of
the heavy book, and I wondered why
there were tears in his eyes. The colonel drew me to him, gently stroked
my short cropped hair, went with me
down the long steps, and told me I
could "go back to the children and
play." I went much more easy in
mind than I came, but it was years
before I comprehended anything
about it.

My studies gave me no trouble, but
I grew very tired, felt hungry all the
time but dared not eat, grew thin and
pale. The colonel noticed it, and
watching me at table found that I was
eating little or nothing, refusing
everything that was offered me. Mistrusting that it was from timidity, he

had food laid on my plate, but I dared
not eat it, and finally at the end of
the term a consultation was held between the colonel, my father and our
beloved family physician, Dr. Delano
Pierce, who lived within a few doors
of the school, and it was decided to
take me home until a little older, and
wiser, I could hope. My timid sen-
sitiveness must have given great annoyance to my friends.   If I ever
could have gotten entirely over it, it
would have given far less annoyance
and trouble to myself all through
life.

To this day, I would rather stand
behind the lines of artillery at Antie-
tam, or cross the pontoon bridge under fire at Fredericksburg, than to
be expected to preside at a public
meeting.

Referring to the breaking up of the first home, and the removal of my father and mother to the new one, it might be well to state the reasons for the change.   A favorite nephew of my father, Mr. Jeremiah Larned, had died after a lingering illness, leaving a widow and four children, from thirteen to six years of age, on the fine farm which had descended to him from his father, Captain Jeremiah Larned, one of the leading men of the town.   Unfortunately, during his long illness the farm had become involved to the extent of necessitating a sale.   This would result in depriving the widow and her small children of a home, and in order to prevent this, and the disadvantages of a creditor's sale, it was decided that my father and a brother-in-law of Mrs.

Larned, Captain Sylvester McIntire,
who had no children, purchase the
farm, and remove there, keeping the
widow and children with them.

The hill farms—for there were two
—were sold to my brothers, who, entering into partnership, constituted the
well known firm of S. & D. Barton,
continuing mainly through their lives.
Thus I became the occupant of two
homes, my sisters remaining with my
brothers, none of whom were married.

The removal to the second home
was a great novelty to me. I became
observant of all changes made. One
of the first things found necessary on
entering a house of such ancient date,
was a rather extensive renovation, for
those days, of painting and papering.
The leading artisan in that line in the

town was Mr. Sylvanus Harris, a courteous man of fine manners, good scholarly acquirements, and who, for nearly half a lifetime, filled the office of town clerk. The records of Oxford will bear his name and his beautiful handwriting as long as its records exist.

Mr. Harris was engaged to make the necessary improvements. Painting included more then than in these later days of prepared material. The painter brought his massive white marble slab, ground his own paints, mixed his colors, boiled his oil, calcined his plaster, made his putty and did scores of things that a painter of to-day would not only never think of doing, but would often scarcely know how to do.

Coming from the newly built house

where I was born, I had seen nothing
of this kind done, and was intensely
interested. I must have persisted in
making myself very numerous, for I
was constantly reminded not to "get
in the gentleman's way." But I was
not to be set aside. My combined interest and curiosity for once overcame my timidity, and encouraged by
the mild, genial face of Mr. Harris,
I gathered the courage to walk up in
front and address him: "Will you
teach me to paint, sir?" "With pleasure, little lady, if mama is willing, I
should very much like your assistance." The consent was forthcoming,
and so was a gown suited to my new
work, and I reported for duty. I
question if any ordinary apprentice
was ever more faithfully and intelli-
gently instructed in his first month's

apprenticeship. I was taught how to
hold my brushes, to take care of them,
allowed to help grind my paints,
shown how to mix and blend them,
how to make putty and use it, to pre-
pare oils and dryings, and learned
from experience that boiling oil was
a great deal hotter than boiling water,
was taught to trim paper neatly, to
match and help to hang it, to make
the most approved paste, and even
varnished the kitchen chairs to the
entire satisfaction of my mother,
which was triumph enough for one
little girl. So interested was I, that
I never wearied of my work for a
day, and at the end of a month looked
on sadly as the utensils, brushes, buck-
ets and great marble slab were taken
away. There was not a room that I
had not helped to make better; there

were no longer mysteries in paint and paper. I knew them all, and that work would bring callouses even on little hands.

When the work was finished and everything gone, I went to my room, lonesome in spite of myself. I found on my candle stand a box containing a pretty little locket, neatly inscribed, "To a faithful worker." No one seemed to have any knowledge of it, and I never gained any.

The new home presented a phase of life quite unfamiliar to me. From never having had any playmates, I now found myself one of a very lively body of six—three boys and three girls nearer of an age than would have been probable in the same family. My father had taken charge of the young

son of a friend—Lovett Stimpson—a
fine, robust, intelligent lad of about
my age, who lived with us.

It would be difficult to describe
what this new life, for the time it continued, became to me, or indeed I to
it. As I look back upon it I realize
that we were a group of good children with honorable instincts, obedient and kindly disposed.   In later
years none of us could recall a serious
difference of any kind, no cruelty and
no broken faith. It took just six, and
no more, to keep a secret. But this por-
trayal of characteristics gives no clue
to, indeed casts no shadow, of what
we were capable of accomplishing in
a day. The territorial domain com-
prised something over three hundred
acres. We knew it all. From "Peakèd
Hill," to "Jim Brown's"—across the

"Flowed Swamp," three miles, we knew every rod of it. Old "Rocky Hills," so high, so steep, so thickly wooded that a horse would never attempt them, were no strangers. We knew where the best chestnuts were. We explored the "Devil's Den," in spite of the tradition that it was an abode for the tempters of Eve. The "French River," that later carried all the factories of North Oxford, spread itself out in lazy rest, after its rugged leaps, as it meandered through the broad, beautiful meadows and interval land, the pride of the farm.

A long hewn log or pole stretched across it in its narrowest, deepest place. I would not dare to say how long, but it could not have been more than fourteen inches wide, and swayed and teetered from the

moment the foot touched till it left it.
The waters glided still and black beneath. It was there as a convenience
for the working men in crossing from
one field to another; but if ever a
week day passed that we did not cross
it several times, we knew one duty
had been neglected. The only saw-
mill in that section of the town was
a part of my father's possessions. The
great up-and-down saw cut its angry
way through the primeval forest
giants from morning till night, and
not unfrequently from night till
morning. The long saw-carriage
ran far out over the raceway at the
rear end. How were we to withstand
the temptation of riding out over the
rushing mill stream twenty feet be-
low, and then coming quickly in as the
sawn log was drawn back for another

cut? Hurt? Never one of us. Killed?
We knew not such a thing could be.

There were three temptingly great
barns, scattered between the house
premises and the interval. Was there
ever a better opportunity for hide-and-
seek, for climbing and jumping? It
would have been no athlete at all that
couldn't jump from the great beams
to the hay, in scant summer time before the new hay came in, and land
on the feet safely. There was, and
still is, directly in front of the house,
a small, circular, natural pond, fed by
springs in the bottom and surrounded
by a cordon of hills forming a basin
in which the little pond basks and
sleeps through the summer, but in
winter becomes a thing of beauty and
a joy forever to the skater. From its
sheltered position it freezes smooth,

even, and glare, and has no danger
spots. I dwell upon this description,
for that little pond was my early love;
the home of my beautiful flock of
graceful ducks.   The boys were all
fine skaters; I wanted to skate, too,
but skating had not then become customary, in fact, not even allowable for
girls; and when, one day, my father
saw me sitting on the ice attempting
to put on a pair of skates, he seemed
shocked, recommended me to the
house, and said something about "tom-
boys."   But this did not cure my desire; nor could I understand why it
was not as well for me to skate as for
the boys; I was as strong, could run
as fast and ride better, indeed they
would not have presumed to approach
me with a horse. Neither could the
boys understand it, and this miscon-

ception led them into an error and me into trouble.

One clear, cold, starlight Sunday morning, I heard a low whistle under my open chamber window. I realized that the boys were out for a skate and wanted to communicate with me. On going to the window, they informed me that they had an extra pair of skates and if I could come out they would put them on me and "learn" me how to skate. It was Sunday morning; no one would be up till late, and the ice was so smooth and "glare." The stars were bright, the temptation was too great. I was in my dress in a moment and out. The skates were fastened on firmly, one of the boy's wool neck "comforters" tied about my waist, to be held by the boy in front. The other two were to stand on either side, and at a signal the cavalcade started.   Swifter and swifter we went, until at length we reached a spot where the ice had been cracked and was full of sharp edges. These threw me, and the speed with which we were progressing, and the distance before we could quite come to a stop, gave terrific opportunity for cuts and wounded knees. The opportunity was not lost. There was more blood flowing than any of us had ever seen. Something must be done. Now all of the wool neck comforters came into requisition; my wounds were bound up, and I was helped into the house, with one knee of ordinary respectable cuts and bruises; the other frightful. Then the enormity of the transaction and its attendant difficulties began to present themselves, and how to surround (for there was no possibility of overcoming them), was the question.

The most feasible way seemed to be to say nothing about it, and we decided to all keep silent; but how to conceal the limp? I must have no limp, but walk well. I managed breakfast without notice. Dinner not quite so well, and I had to acknowledge that I had slipped down and hurt my knee a little. This gave my limp more latitude, but the next day it was so decided, that I was held up and searched. It happened that the best knee was inspected; the stiff wool comforter soaked off, and a suitable dressing given it. This was a great relief, as it afforded pretext for my limp, no one observing that I limped with the wrong knee.

But the other knee was not a wound to heal by first intention, especially under its peculiar dressing, and finally had to be revealed. The result was a surgical dressing and my foot held up in a chair for three weeks, during which time I read the "Arabian Nights" from end to end. As the first dressing was finished, I heard the surgeon say to my father: "that was a hard case, Captain, but she stood it like a soldier." But when I saw how genuinely they all pitied, and how tenderly they nursed me, even walking lightly about the house not to jar my swollen and fevered limbs, in spite of my disobedience and detestable deception (and persevered in at that), my Sabbath breaking and unbecoming conduct, and all the trouble I had caused, conscience revived, and my

mental suffering far exceeded my
physical. The Arabian Nights were
none too powerful a soporific to hold
me in reasonable bounds. I despised
myself and failed to sleep or eat.

My mother, perceiving my re-
morseful condition, came to the rescue, telling me soothingly, that she
did not think it the worst thing that
could have been done, that other little
girls had probably done as badly, and
strengthened her conclusions by telling me how she once persisted in riding a high mettled unbroken horse in
opposition to her father's commands,
and was thrown. My supposition is
that she had been a worthy mother of
her equestrian son.

The lesson was not lost on any of
the group.   It is very certain that
none of us, boys or girls, indulged in

further smart tricks. Twenty-five years later, when on a visit to the old home, long left, I saw my father, then a grey-haired grandsire, out on the same little pond, fitting the skates carefully to the feet of his little twin granddaughters, holding them up to make their first start in safety, I remembered my wounded knees, and blessed the great Father that progress and change were among the possibilities of His people.

I never learned to skate. When it became fashionable I had neither time nor opportunity.

Along these lines I recall another disappointment, which, though not vital, was still indicative of the times. During the following winter a dancing school was opened in the hall of

the one hotel on Oxford Plain, some
three miles from us. It was taught
by a personal friend of my father, a
polished gentleman, resident of a
neighboring town, and teacher of English schools. By some chance I got a
glimpse of the dancing school at the
opening, and was seized with a most
intense desire to go and learn to
dance. With my peculiar characteristics it was necessary for me to want
a thing very much before mentioning
it; but this overcame me, especially
as the cordial teacher took tea
with us one evening before going
to his school, and spoke very in-
terestingly of his classes. I even
went so far as to beg permission
to go. The dance was in my very
feet. The violin haunted me. "Ladies change" and "all hands round"

sounded in my ears and woke me from my sleep at night.

The matter was taken up in family council. I was thought to be very young to be allowed to go to a dancing school in a hotel. Dancing at that time was at a very low ebb in good New England society, and besides, there was an active revival taking place in both of the orthodox churches (or rather one a church and the other a society without a church), and it might not be a wise, nor even a courteous, thing to allow. Not that our family, with its well known liberal proclivities, could have the slightest objection on that score; still, like St. Paul, if meat were harmful to their brethren they would not eat it, and thus it was decided that I could not go. The decision was

perfectly conscientious, kindness itself, and probably wise; but I have
wondered if they could have known
(as they never did) how severe the
disappointment was, the tears it cost
me in my little bed in the dark, the
music and the master's voice still
sounding in my ears, if this knowledge would have weighed in the decision.

I have listened to a great deal of
music since then, interspersed with
very positive orders, and which generally called for "all hands round" but
the dulcet notes of the violin and the
"ladies change" were missing. Neither
did I ever learn to dance.

From the peculiar gifts that were
wont to be made me in those days, I
am led to infer that my peculiarities

in the direction of the dumb animal
part of creation, were decidedly no-
ticeable.   On one occasion an English gentleman, a friend of the family, and, like my father, a promoter of
fine stock, had been paying us a visit,
and upon returning to his home, near
Boston, sent to me a beautifully soft,
wool-wadded basket containing two
and a half dozens of fine, large duck's
eggs.   It was not difficult to find
among the numerous feathered inhab-
itants of the barns, three domestically
inclined, motherly hens, willing to
take charge of the big tinted eggs, al-
beit not their own, giving to them the
strictest attention.   The result was,
that within four weeks, the shallow
end of the little pond was covered
with tiny balls of yellow down float-
ing calmly and majestically on the

water—darting rapidly this way and
that, for every fly or bug so unfortu-
nate as to appear, while the shore presented the scene of three of the most
distracted mothers that imagination
can picture. There was nothing majestic nor calm in their motions, and
the tones which called the recreant
broods were far from soothing; but
like the mothers of other wayward,
unnatural offspring, the lesson of sub-
mission was theirs to learn; and
through resignation at length came
peace.

In the course of two or three years
my flock of ducks became so numerous as to attract the attention of the
wild ducks, passing over from the
northern lakes to the southern bays,
and it was no uncommon thing for
an entire flock, wearied with a long

journey, to alight for a few days' rest. My tame ducks learned athletics from these native divers and dippers, and the scene became at times not only interesting, but inspiring and instructive.

It is very evident to me, as I remember it, that my aspirations were by no means satisfied with an interest in these small specimens, such as ducks, hens, turkeys, geese, dogs, cats, etc., of which I had no lack. This not including canaries, of which I received from time to time a number as gifts; but I had no pleasure in them, and although doubtless the most inhuman thing that could have been done, I invariably opened the cage door and let them out.

But all that farm land, the three great barns and accompanying yards,

called for cattle.   A small herd of
twenty-five fine milch cows came
faithfully home each day with the
lowering of the sun, for the milking
and extra supper which they knew
awaited them.   With the customary
greed of childhood I had laid claim to
three or four of the handsomest and
tamest of them, and believing myself to be their real owner, I went
faithfully every evening to the yards
to receive and look after them.   My
little milk pail went as well, and I
became proficient in an art never forgotten.

One afternoon, on going to the barn
as usual, I found no cows there; all
had been driven somewhere else.   As
I stood in the corner of the great yard
alone, I saw three or four men—the
farm hands—with one stranger among

them wearing a long, loose shirt or gown. They were all trying to get a large red ox onto the barn floor, to which he went very reluctantly. At length they succeeded. One of the men carried an axe, and stepping a little to the side and back, raised it high in the air and brought it down with a terrible blow. The ox fell, I fell too; and the next I knew I was in the house on a bed, and all the family about me, with the traditional camphor bottle, bathing my head to my great discomfort. As I regained consciousness they asked me what made me fall? I said "some one struck me." "Oh, no," they said, "no one struck you," but I was not to be convinced and proceeded to argue the case with an impatient putting away of the hurting hands, "then what makes my head so sore?" Happy ignorance! I had not then learned the mystery of nerves.

I have, however, a very clear recollection of the indignation of my father (my mother had already expressed herself on the subject), on his return from town and hearing what had taken place. The hired men were lined up and arraigned for "cruel carelessness." They had "the consideration to keep the cattle away," he said, "but allowed that little girl to stand in full view." Of course, each protested he had not seen me. I was altogether too friendly with the farm hands to hear them blamed, especially on my account, and came promptly to their side, assuring my father that they had not seen me, and that it was "no matter," I was "all well now."

But, singularly, I lost all desire for meat, if I had ever had it—and all through life to the present, have only eaten it when I must for the sake of appearance, or as circumstances seemed to make it the more proper thing to do. The bountiful ground has always yielded enough for all my needs and wants.

I had been eleven years old the Christmas before. Great changes had taken place during the two or three preceding years. My energetic brothers had outgrown farming, sold their two farms on the hill, and come down and bought of my father all his water power on the French River, as well as all obtainable timber land in the vicinity. The staunch old up-and-down saw still stood in its majesty

for the handling of the forest giants
too massive for a lesser power, but it
was surrounded by a cordon of belt-
ed "circulars," whirling with a speed
that quite obscured their motion,
screaming, screeching and throwing
out the product of their work in all
directions; shingles, laths, thin boards,
bolters and slitters. New dams had
been thrown across the shifty, flighty
stream, to be swept away in the tor-
rents of the spring freshets and float-
ing ice, but replaced at once with
an obstinate manliness and enterprise
that scarcely admitted of an interrup-
tion in the work.

In a new building along the side of
the dam, the great burr-stones of that
date ground out the wholesome grain
of all the surrounding country, and
where I had first seen it under the

control of the one lone sawyer, now fifty of the strongest working men that could be procured, and great four-horse teams covered the once quiet millyard.   The entire line of factories above had caught the inspiration, and the French River villages of North Oxford were models of growth and activity.

One sister had married and settled in her home near by, and a wife had come into my eldest brother's home. Mrs. Larned, the widow to whose assistance my father had gone in her early desolation, had found her children now so well grown as to make it advisable to remove to one of the factory villages, where she became a popular boarding house keeper, and her children operatives in the mill.

Thus, I was again left to myself.

The schools were not the best, but all
that could be done for me, in or out
of them, was done. I had been especially well taught to sew and liked
it, but knitting was beyond me. I
could not be held to it, and it was
given up.

Through the confirmed invalidism
of my elder sister, Dorothea, I lost
her beautiful guidance, but the watch-
ful care of my younger sister, now
Mrs. Vassall, was truly pathetic. She
never lost sight of my welfare, and
her fine literary taste was a constant
inspiration.

While thus in the midst of my various pursuits and vocations, an acci-
dental turn in my wheel of fortune
changed my entire course (for a time
at least) and how much bearing, if

any, it may have had on the future,
I have never been able to determine.
I have spoken of the younger of my
two brothers, of the firm of S. &
D. Barton, as a fine horseman. He
was more than that. In these days
he would have been an athlete. The
two men were but two years apart in
age, of fine disposition and excellent
physical strength, integrity and courage; of fine disposition and equable
temper; yet neither of them men with
whom an opponent would carelessly
or tauntingly covet an encounter. The
younger, David, from his physical activity and daring, was always selected
for any feat of danger to be per-
formed.

These were days when even build-
ings were "raised by hand." All the
neighborhood was expected to partic-

ipate in a "raising." Upon one occasion, an uncommonly large barn,
with what was then still more uncommon, a cellar beneath, was to be raised.
The rafters must be affixed to the ridge-
pole, and David Barton was assigned
to this duty. While in its performance, a timber on which he was standing, having been weakened by an unobserved knot, suddenly gave way,
and he fell directly to the first floor,
striking on his feet on another timber
near the bottom of the cellar. Without
falling he leaped to the ground, and
after a few breathless minutes declared himself unhurt, but was not
permitted to return aloft.   It was
spoken of as a "remarkable adven-
ture," "a wonderful escape," etc., and
for a few days all went well, with the
exception of a slight and quite unac-

customed headache, which continued
to increase as the July weather pro-
gressed. At length he showed symp-
toms of fever; the family physician
was called, and here commenced a
system of medical treatment quite un-
known to our physicians of the present day, other than as results of historical research and milestones of
scientific advancement.

He was pronounced in a "settled
fever," which must not be "broken
up," and could only be held in check
by reducing the strength of the patient.   He had "too much blood,"
was "too vigorous," "just the patient
for a fever to 'go hard with,' " it was
said.   Accordingly, the blood was
taken from time to time, as long as
it seemed safe to do so.   The terrible
pain in the head continued and blis-

ters were applied to all possible places,
in the hope of withdrawing the pain.
Sleepless, restless, in agony both
physical and mental, his case grew
desperate.   He had been my ideal
from earliest memory.   I was distressed beyond measure at his condition. I had been his little protégée,
his companion, and in his nervous
wretchedness he clung to me. Thus,
from the first days and nights of illness, I remained near his side. The
fever ran on and over all the traditional turning points, seven, fourteen,
twenty-one days. I could not be taken
away from him except by compulsion,
and he was unhappy until my return.
I learned to take all directions for his
medicines from his physician (who
had eminent counsel) and to admin-
ister them like a genuine nurse.

My little hands became schooled to
the handling of the great, loathsome,
crawling leeches which were at first
so many snakes to me, and no fingers
could so painlessly dress the angry
blisters; and thus it came about, that
I was the accepted and acknowledged
nurse of a man almost too ill to re-
cover.

Finally, as the summer passed, the
fever gave way, and for a wonder the
patient did not.   No physician will
doubt that I had given him poison
enough to have killed him many times
over, if suitably administered with
that view.   He will also understand
the condition in which the patient was
left.   They had certainly succeeded in
reducing his strength.

Late in the autumn he stood on his
feet for the first time since July. Still

sleepless, nervous, cold, dyspeptic—a mere wreck of his former self. None were so disturbed over his condition as his kind-hearted, and for those days, skillful physicians, who had exhausted their knowledge and poured out their sympathy and care like water, on the patient who, for his manliness and bravery, they had come to respect, and for his suffering learned to love with a parent's tenderness.

It now became a matter of time. Councils of physicians for twenty miles around sat in judgment on the case. They could only recommend; and more blisters, setons and various methods of external irritation for the withdrawal of internal pain followed, from month to month and season to season. All these were my preferred care.

I realize now how carefully and apprehensively the whole family watched the little nurse, but I had no idea of it then. I thought my position the most natural thing in the world; I almost forgot that there was an outside to the house.

This state of things continued with little change—a trifling gain of strength in my patient at times—for two years, when, entirely unexpected, the most tabooed and little known of all medical treatments, restored him to health. It is to be remembered at that date there was no homeopathy, no hydropathy, no sanitariums, no Christian Science, nothing but the regular school of allopathic medicine. Medical practitioners, baffled by lack of science, surrounded by ignorance on all such subjects and more or less of superstition, struggled manfully on toward the blessed light of the scientific knowledge of to-day, which they have so richly attained.

It was not to be wondered at that the slightest departure from the beaten track, under these conditions, was held as unpardonable and punishable quackery; and that the first "ism" that broke through the defense fought the fight of a forlorn hope. There are young physicians of good historical knowledge to-day, who have never learned that "Thompsonianism" was that "ism"; that Dr. Samuel Thompson fought that fight, and that they are pursuing many excellent methods which are the result of his thought; that it was he who first advanced the theory (in this country at least,) that fever was not the foe, but the friend

of the patient; that it was simply un-
equal animal warmth and vigor—that
people did not have too much blood
any more than they had too much
bone, and could as ill afford to lose
it; that if the blood were too thick,
or too thin, or of a bad quality, taking away a portion of it would not
rectify or purify the remainder. That
a blister was not likely to soothe a
nervous patient to sleep, or to extract
a pain, save by creating a greater. But
that a better way to treat disturbances
was to open the pores generally, by a
vapor bath—designated "Thompson's
Steam Box," and greatly to be feared.
He and his few followers were
known as "Steam Doctors"—and the
public warned against them.

It happened that one of his disci-
ples, a "Steam Doctor," residing in a

neighboring town (I will write his name in grateful remembrance—Dr. Asa McCullum), had watched this remarkable case with interest and pity, convinced that the right remedies had not reached it.

He ventured at length to approach my father on the subject; then my brother, who was willing to attempt anything short of suicide. The result was the removal of the patient to the home asylum of the doctor for treatment. In three weeks he was so far restored as to return home and take his place in his business, like one come back from the dead. I remember the greetings—the tears of gladness on the blessed face of our family physician when he came to welcome him home: "And so, David, something good has come out of Nazareth."

I was again free; my occupation
gone. Life seemed very strange and
idle to me. I wondered that my
father took me to ride so much, and
that my mother hoped she could make
me some new clothes now, for in the
two years I had not grown an inch,
had been to school one-half day, and
had gained one pound in weight.

This singular mode of life, at so
young an age, could not have been
without its characteristic effects. In
some respects it had served to height-
en serious defects. The seclusion had
increased the troublesome bashfulness.
I had grown even more timid, shrink-
ing and sensitive in the presence of
others; absurdly careful and method-
ical for a child; afraid of giving
trouble by letting my wants be known,
thereby giving the very pain I sought

to avoid, and instead of feeling that my freedom gave me time for recreation or play, it seemed to me like time wasted, and I looked anxiously about for some useful occupation.

As usual, my blessed sister, Mrs. Vassall, came to the rescue. Taking advantage of an all-absorbing love of poetry (which I always had) she made a weapon of it by providing me with the poetical works of Walter Scott, which I had not read, and proposed that we read them together. We naturally commenced with "The Lady of the Lake." I was immediately transported to the Highlands and the Bonny Braes, plucking the heather and broom and guiding the skiff across Loch Katrine, listening to the sweet warning song of poor crazed Blanche of Devon, thrilling with,

"Saxon, I am Roderick Dhu," and trudging along with the old minstrel and Ellen to Sterling tower and the Court of Fitz-James. "Marmion" followed, and then all the train of English poetry that a child could take in.

My second individual ownership was "Billy." His personality (which I never questioned), was represented by a high stepping brown Morgan horse, with glossy coat, slim legs, pointed ears, long curly black mane and tail, and weighing nearly nine hundred pounds.

Although a good driver, his forte was the saddle. His gait (or rather, I should say, gaits) was first a delightful single-foot; but which he had the faculty of changing to a rack, or pace or trot, as occasion or haste seemed

to call for; and as a last resort, he
could cover them all by something one
does not like to name; but we only
used that gait on extraordinary occa-
sions. My father had purchased and
given Billy to me when about ten
years old. The same figures will do
for us both.

I had three or four neighboring girl
associates who also had their own or
family horses, and our riding parties
were the events of the season. An-
ticipating the deep, forbidding snows
of the winter in New England, we
had the custom of celebrating
Thanksgiving day by a final party
for the season. Even this was
cold and had often some traces
of snow.

On the present occasion there were
but three of us, Martha, Eveline and

myself.   Martha had a fine sorrel
trotter, Eveline a spirited single-
footer. The day was cold and threat-
ening. Our ride was to Worcester,
some ten miles.   When about three
miles from home, on our return, a
blinding snowstorm set in, literally
a gale. This either frightened or ex-
cited Eveline's horse, which, master-
ing the situation by a quick toss of the
head, and catch of the bit (a trick he
evidently understood), dropped his
single-foot as something adapted to
ladies and little girls, and fell to us-
ing all the feet he had, the best he
knew. Awed by her peril, but pow-
erless to aid, we could only follow our
fleeing comrade to be ready to help
when she should fall, as we were sure
she must.   The gale mercilessly increased; so did our speed. We kept

nearly alongside, every horse upon the "dead run."

We must have presented a striking miniature picture of the veritable "Three Furies" on a rampage. A country road and no one passing. Martha and myself each rushing directly past our own homes unobserved in the storm, till at length we rounded the curve that brought the flying horse in sight of his own stable. They had sighted the coming cavalcade. The gates were thrown wide open, and a man stationed on either side to catch both horse and rider when they should enter.

Seeing the worn-out girl once safely in her father's arms, we turned away, with an entirely new chapter added to our very limited stock of equestrian knowledge. We were all alive and unharmed, and I alone am here now to tell the little stories of childhood's terrifying dangers and miraculous escapes.

We were midway between the two district schools, a long mile and a half from either, and it frequently chanced that a season or two of indifferent schools followed each other in train. The experiment of sending me away to school was not to be repeated, and accordingly I was undertaken at home. My mathematical brother, Stephen, took charge of that department, and Mrs. Vassall the other needful studies, while my former patient, brother David, the equestrian of early days, now grown strong and well, kept to his rule of practical teaching. I recall vividly the half impatient

frown on his fine face when he would
see me do an awkward thing, however
trivial. He detested false motions;
wanted the thing done rightly the
first time. If I started to go somewhere, go, and not turn back; if to
do something, do it. I must throw a
ball or a stone with an under swing
like a boy and not a girl, and must
make it go where I sent it, and not
fall at my feet and foolishly laugh at
it. If I would drive a nail, strike it
fairly on the head every time, and not
split the board. If I would draw a
screw, turn it right the first time. I
must tie a square knot that would hold,
and not tie my horse with a slip noose
and leave him to choke himself. These
were little things, still a part of the
instructions not to be undervalued. In
the rather practical life which has

sometimes fallen to me, I have wondered if they were not among the most useful, and if that handsome frown were not one of my best lessons.

At length there came a school that could be utilized, and my family instructors were relieved. The school to the north of us was undertaken by Mr. Lucian Burleigh, a younger member of the noted Burleigh family, and brother of William H. Burleigh, the poet. It seemed very strange to me to be in school again. I had been so long accustomed to govern myself, in a manner, that I wondered how any one should need others to govern them. If scholars came there to learn, why should they try, or want, to do anything else? There is no doubt that I seemed equally unaccountable and prudish to them.

MR. JONATHAN DANA,
MY OXFORD TEACHER.

The quick perceptions of the teacher at once comprehended the conditions, and he treated me with the greatest consideration and kindness; advising such changes and additions as seemed suitable, and most in accord with the studies I had taken with me; even, as I could later see, forming some new classes in branches outside of the customary routine of the public school; as elementary astronomy, ancient history, and the "Science of Language"; his own literary and scholarly tastes pointing significantly to the latter. If Milton's "Paradise Lost," and Pollok's "Course of Time" were ever dissected, transposed, analyzed and "parsed" by any class of vigilant youths, it was then and there.

The winter passed all too soon. A mile and a half through the snow had been only a pleasure. Our faithful, brotherly teacher left us, never to return; but the still brotherly friendship between teacher and pupil remained unbroken until his summons came.

After a busy summer a similarly good fortune awaited me in the next winter term of school. Mr. Jonathan Dana, one of Oxford's most scholarly men and a teacher of note, commenced the winter school to the south of us. I have no words to describe the value of his instruction, nor the pains he took with his eager pupil. I had been far too thoroughly drilled to require time for the customary classes of the public school, but did require instruction in branches forbidden in their lawful curriculum.

In spite of the labor of a school of sixty pupils of all ages, with no as-

sistant, I was permitted to take phil-
osophy, chemistry and elementary
Latin—all to be taught outside of
school hours. With no laboratory at
hand, I have often marveled at the
amount of experimental instruction
he found it possible to give me. So
generally appreciated was the excel-
lence of the school that the term was
continued beyond the customary three
months. My grateful homage for my
inestimable teacher and his interest in
his early pupil, became memories of a
lifetime, and the social acquaintance
was never interrupted until the late
summons came to him, white haired
and venerable, to go up higher.

My family were all gratified by my
progress and my deportment as a
student, but I was still diffident, timid,
non-committal, afraid of giving

trouble and difficult to understand. My physical growth had not met their expectations nor their hopes. I grew slowly and was still a "little girl" in appearance. This went to show how positive the early check had been, and how slowly the repairs were made, for it was said that I gained an inch in height between the ages of twenty and twenty-one.

The firm of my brothers, S. & D. Barton, had added to their ever increasing business the manufacture of cloth. A factory had been erected and a partnership entered into with Messrs. Paul and Samuel Parsons, two elegant gentlemen among the earlier manufacturers of satinet in this country, and the new factory was known as "The Satinet Mill of North

Oxford." A very superior article of
cloth was made, the operatives almost
entirely American, and very largely
from families of the neighborhood or
surrounding country.   Occupations
for women were few in those days,
and often the school and music teacher, weary of the monotonous life,
sought change in the more remunera-
tive loom of the factory.   I name this
as a matter of history, as the North
Oxford Mills were the third, if not
the second after Slater, who produced
the first spindle and power looms in
America, at the risk of his life.

I had been taken through the new
factory by my brother; had seen these
young persons at work; watched the
shuttles fly under the deft fingers of
the weavers, and felt that there was
something I could do.   There was no

school, I was idle. After a little quiet reflection I astonished the family by announcing my desire to go into the mill. I wanted to weave cloth. At first they tried laughing at me. I was too sensitive to be dealt with in that way. Then reasoning. I was "too small"; it was not a proper thing for me to do. But I was not easily dissuaded. One day in the midst of a family council, my brother Stephen chanced to call. He listened attentively, saw that I was anxious and troubled, and was giving trouble to others as well. At length he spoke. Addressing my mother, he said: "I do not see anything so very much out of the way in the request. I wonder if we are not drawing the lines too tightly on our little sister? A few years ago she wanted to learn to dance; this was denied as frivolous and improper; now she asks to work. She took up a work by herself and did it two years, a work that no child would be expected to do, and did it well. She is certainly a properly behaved little girl, and I cannot understand why we should trouble ourselves or her so much concerning the proprieties of her life. For my part, I am very willing to arrange a pair of looms for her and let her try." A hush fell on the group. My anxious mother seemed relieved. The big brother had spoken. I crept shyly up under his stalwart arm and kissed his bearded cheek.

The next day a low platform was run along in front of a pair of new, glossy looms, just by the desk of the overseer of the room. A good weaver

was given charge to instruct me, and
when I stepped upon that platform
and looked down upon the evenly
drawn warp and the swiftly flying
shuttles, and felt that they were mine,
I imagine the sensation was akin to
that of a young queen whose foot first
presses the throne. I was too carefully watched to permit a mistake,
and too interested to be tired. Before
the end of the week I was able to dis-
charge my instructress, or it is more
probable she discharged herself in
view of my self-sufficiency. I could
scarcely wait in the morning for the
bell to call me, early as it would be,
and I walked up that long, outside
flight of black, greasy stairs and entered that whirring, clashing room
with as much pride and satisfaction
as I would have entered the finest and

most highly embellished schoolroom.
I observed that the help all looked
at me as I went in, and McDonald, the
overseer, always raised his Scotch cap
a bit by the tassel, or touched his fin-
ger to the rim, fitting so closely to
his high forehead.   I thought I ought
to make some acknowledgement of
this, and always did so, but could not
understand it.   I told my mother
about it and asked her what he did
it for?   She said that it was probably
because I was "so little."   That perhaps if I were as large as the other
girls he might not do it.   I thought
this a reasonable solution and was satisfied.

I finished my first week, commenced
my second, and went through with no
assistance.   On Saturday my webs
were cut from the looms, examined

and pronounced of first quality, show-
ing great care. I took my proud rec-
ord home. The next day (Sunday),
Mr. Samuel Parsons, with the prudent
care that could not trust even the
watchman too implicitly, went into the
mill by himself, ascending to the
picker room in the top story, where
the light, oiled wool was piled in
great quantities. He casually placed
his hand upon it in passing, and observing that it felt warm, he plunged
his arm in to lift it. The flames en-
veloped him. He ran at full speed
the length of the building to the bell
rope. The fire was there almost before him. He gave two strokes, when
the flames drove him from the room;
they licked down the air shafts and
belt holes, lapping up the oil like so
much food, as it was.

The perfection of the magnificent fire departments of the present day was far in the future then. In three hours it was all over, and the new North Oxford Satinet Mills were a smoking pile of rubbish, a thing of the past. No heart was heavier than mine. The strong, energetic brothers knew that rebuilding would commence at once, but I mourned without hope.

If ever there were lost or omitted a well-turned joke or a bit of humor by the various members of the Barton family it was clearly an accident, no such omission being ever intended; and thus it was suggested to me, that, as the fire was manifestly a case of spontaneous combustion, could it have been that I worked so fast that the friction set the mill on fire? That joke on me lasted many years. The mill was rebuilt, as well as several others, some to be burned, some to be sold; but I had found other occupations more congenial to the other members of the household, it is to be hoped, if not to me.

The recital of this incident by myself, or some one else, has given rise to the bit of romance cropping out occasionally, in the sketches one sees, that I was a factory girl and earned the money to pay off the mortgage on my father's farm. I wish the first statement might have been true. Nothing to-day would gratify me more than to know that I had been one of those self-reliant, intelligent, American-born girls like our sweet poetess, Lucy Larcom, and like her had stood before the power looms in the early progress of the manufactories of our great and matchless country. I fear that my plain, simple facts will rob many a fancy sketch of its brightest tints, as in this instance. I am compelled to confess in regard to the second statement, that my father never had a mortgage that I knew of, and, therefore, had no need of my brave help.   On the other hand, he had something to give to me.

I think it usually occurs in small communities that there is one family, or one house, to which all strangers or new comers naturally gravitate. Nothing was plainer than that ours was that house. All lecturers, upon any subject, clergymen on trial, whoever had a new idea to expound and was in need of an abiding place meanwhile, found one there. My father's

active and liberal mind inclined him
to examination and toleration, and his
cordial hospitality was seconded by
my mother's welcome to any one who
could bring new thought or culture to
herself or her family.

These were the very earliest days of
phrenology. The famous brothers,
O. S. and L. N. Fowler, worthy dis-
ciples of Spurzheim and Coombe,
were commencing their lifelong
work. Young men of advanced ideas,
thought, energy and purpose.

The "Phrenological Journal," if
existing at all, was in its infancy. The
Fowler brothers were among the
most interesting and popular lecturers in the country. Two courses of
lectures by L. N. Fowler were arranged for our town; one for North
and the other for South Oxford, or

"Oxford Plain," as it is better known. He very naturally became the guest of my father and mother.

These two courses of lectures covered nearly a month of time. How can the value of the results of that month, extending through a lifetime, be put into words? How measure the worth of the ideas, the knowledge of one's self, and of others, growing out of it? Aside from this was his aid and comfort to my mother in her perplexity concerning her incomprehensible child. I recall the long, earnest talks, in which it was evident that I was the prime subject, although not clearly realizing it at the time. Upon one occasion there was no question. I was ill (of mumps, I believe) and to avoid loneliness was permitted to lie on the lounge in the large sitting room

through the day.   Forgetting my
presence, or believing me asleep, the
conversation went on in my hearing,
portions of which at this late day I
recall.   My mother remarked that
none of her children had ever been so
difficult to manage. "Was I disobe-
dient, exacting or wayward?" asked
Mr. Fowler.   Oh no! she often
wished I were, she would then know
what to do, for I would make my
wants known, and they could be supplied.   But I was so timid and afraid
of making trouble that they were in
constant fear of neglecting me; I
would do without the most needed article rather than ask for it, and my
bashfulness increased rather than di-
minished as I grew older. As an illus-
tration, she stated that only last Sunday the child appeared with bare

hands when we were ready for church. Upon being asked where were her gloves, she reluctantly replied that she "had none. They were worn out." Upon being asked why she had not said so and asked for others, the reply was a burst of tears and an attempt to leave the room. "We would not permit this unhappy day at home alone, and took her as she was," said my mother. All this sounded very badly to me as I heard it rehearsed. It was all true, all wrong; would I, could I ever learn to do better?

Mr. Fowler replied that these characteristics were all indicated; that, however much her friends might suffer from them, she would always suffer more. "They may be apparently outgrown, but the sensitive nature will always remain. She will never

assert herself for herself—she will suffer wrong first—but for others she
will be perfectly fearless." To my
mother's anxious question, "what shall
I do?" he replied, "Throw responsibility upon her. She has all the quali-
ties of a teacher. As soon as her age
will permit, give her a school to
teach." I well remember how this
suggestion shocked me. I should not
have remembered all these advices,
but years after they were found with
much more among my mother's carefully preserved papers; some corre-
spondence must have followed. The
depth and faithfulness of the interest
felt, was shown in the fact that the
great reader of human character,
through his long life in foreign lands
as well as his own, never forgot the
troublesome child. Occasional cor-

respondence and valued meetings across the sea marked the milestones of life, till one road came to an end. A great and true man and friend of humanity had gone, and the world was better for his having lived in it.

At the close of the second term of school, the advice was acted upon, and it was arranged that I teach the school in District No. 9. My sister resided within the district. How well I remember the preparations—the efforts to look larger and older, the examination by the learned committee of one clergyman, one lawyer and one justice of the peace; the certificate with "excellent" added at the close; the bright May morning over the dewy, grassy road to the schoolhouse, neither large nor new, and not a pupil in sight.

On entering, I found my little
school of forty pupils all seated ac-
cording to their own selection, quietly
waiting with folded hands.   Bright,
rosy-cheeked boys and girls from four
to thirteen, with the exception of four
lads, as tall and nearly as old as myself. These four boys naturally looked
a little curiously at me, as if forming
an opinion of how best to dispose of
me, as rumor had it that on the preceding summer, not being *en rapport*
with the young lady teacher, they had
excluded her from the building and
taken   possession   themselves.   All
arose as I entered, and remained
standing until requested to sit. Never
having observed how schools were
opened, I was compelled, as one
would say, to "blaze my own way."
I was too timid to address them, but

holding my Bible, I said they might
take their Testaments and turn to the
Sermon on the Mount.   All who
could read, read a verse each, I reading with them in turn. This opened
the way for remarks upon the mean-
ing of what they had read. I found
them more ready to express themselves than I had expected, which was
helpful to me as well. I asked them
what they supposed the Saviour meant
by saying that they must love their
enemies and do good to them that
hated and misused them? This was a
hard question, and they hesitated, until at length a little bright-eyed girl
with great earnestness replied: "I
think He meant that you must be good
to everybody, and mustn't quarrel nor
make nobody feel bad, and I'm going to try." An ominous smile crept

over the rather hard faces of my four
lads, but my response was so prompt,
and my approval so hearty, that it dis-
appeared and they listened attentively
but ventured no remarks. With this
moderate beginning the day pro-
gressed, and night found us social,
friendly and classed for a school.
Country schools did not admit of
home dinners. I also remained. On
the second or third day an accident
on their outside field of rough play
called me to them. They had been
playing unfairly and dangerously and
needed teaching, even to play well. I
must have thought they required object lessons, for almost imperceptibly
either to them or to myself, I joined
in the game and was playing with
them.

My four lads soon perceived that I

was no stranger to their sports or
their tricks; that my early education
had not been neglected, and that they
were not the first boys I had seen.
When they found that I was as agile
and as strong as themselves, that my
throw was as sure and as straight as
theirs, and that if they won a game
it was because I permitted it, their
respect knew no bounds. No cour-
tesy within their knowledge was neglected. Their example was sufficient
for the entire school. I have seen no
finer type of boys. They were faithful to me in their boyhood, and in
their manhood faithful to their country. Their blood crimsoned its hard-
est fields, and the little bright-eyed
girl with the good resolve, has made
her whole life a blessing to others,
and still lives to follow the teaching

given her. Little Emily has "made nobody feel bad."

My school was continued beyond the customary length of time, and its only hard feature was our parting. In memory I see that pitiful group of children sobbing their way down the hill after the last good-bye was said, and I was little better. We had all been children together, and when, in accordance with the then custom at town meetings, the grades of the schools were named and No. 9 stood first for discipline, I thought it the greatest injustice, and remonstrated, affirming that there had been no discipline, that not one scholar had ever been disciplined. Child that I was, I did not know that the surest test of discipline is its absence.

If the published school report, so

misunderstood by me, had given me
displeasure, it had also given me a
local reputation, quite as unexpected.
I soon found myself the recipient of
numerous invitations to teach in the
nearby towns, especially such schools
as required the "discipline" so largely
accredited to, and so little deserved,
by me.

Declination, on my part, was not
to be thought of. All members of the
family were only too grateful for the
progress I had made towards proper
self-assurance to permit any back-
sliding, and it was early settled that I
accept the application of the honorable
committee, to teach the next summer
school at what was known as the
"Mill-ward" in the adjoining town of
Charlton, commencing on the first
Monday in May of the following year

—a "master" teaching the winter term.

One day, early in September, my brother David, now one of the active, popular business men of the town, nearly took my breath away by inviting me to accompany him on a journey to the state of Maine, to be present at his wedding and with him bring back the wife who was to grace his home and share his future life.

There was now more lengthening of skirts, and a rush of dressmaking such as I had never known before; and when, two weeks later, I found myself with my brother and a rather gay party of ladies and gentlemen, friends of his, at one of the most elegant hotels in Boston (where I had never been) waiting the arrival of a de-

layed steamer, I was so overcome by
the dread of committing some impro-
priety or indiscretion which might
embarrass my brother that I begged
him to permit me to go back home.
I was not distressed about what might
be thought of *me*. I did not seem to
care much about that; but how it
might reflect upon my brother, and
the mortification that my awkward-
ness could not fail to inflict on him.

I had never set foot on a vessel
or seagoing craft of any kind, and
when, in the glitter of that finely
equipped steamer, I really crossed
over a corner of the great Atlantic
ocean, the very waves of which
touched other continents as well, I
felt that my world was miraculously
widening.

It was another merry party, and

magnificent spans of horses that met and galloped away with us over the country to our destination.

But the crowning astonishment came when I was informed that it was the desire and decision of all parties, that I act as bridesmaid. That I assist in introducing the younger of the guests, and stand beside the tall, handsome young bride who was to be my sister, while she pledged her troth to the brother dearer to me than my own life.

This responsibility seemed to throw the whole world wide open to me. How well I remember the tearful resolution with which I pledged myself to try to overcome my troublesome propensities and to strive only for the courage of the right, and for the fearlessness of true womanhood so much

DAVID BARTON.
MY YOUNGER BROTHER AND RIDING MASTER.

needed and earnestly desired, and so painfully lacking.

November found us home again. Under the circumstances, there must naturally be a share of social gayeties during the winter, and some preparations for my new school duties; and I waited with more or less apprehension for what would be my first life among strangers, and the coming of my anticipated "First of May." With slight variation I could have joined truthfully in the dear old child refrain:

> "Then wake and call me early,
>   Call me early, mother dear,"
> For that will be the veriest day
> "Of all the glad New Year."